ABANDONED
MIAMI

ABANDONED
MIAMI
STAY OUT

TANYA VELAZCO

America Through Time is an imprint of Fonthill Media LLC
www.through-time.com
office@through-time.com

Published by Arcadia Publishing by arrangement with Fonthill Media LLC
For all general information, please contact Arcadia Publishing:
Telephone: 843-853-2070
Fax: 843-853-0044
E-mail: sales@arcadiapublishing.com
For customer service and orders:
Toll-Free 1-888-313-2665

www.arcadiapublishing.com

First published 2019

Copyright © Tanya Velazco 2019

ISBN 978-1-63499-124-7

Typeset in Trade Gothic 10pt on 15pt
Printed and bound in England

CONTENTS

Introduction **9**

1 Captain Burke's Castle **11**

2 Al Capone's House **39**

3 The Redlinger Orchids Ornamental Nursery **52**

4 Boca Murder House **79**

5 UFO House **101**

6 Unknown Coral Rock Home **115**

Afterword **122**

Endnotes **124**

Bibliography **126**

This book is dedicated to my beautiful daughter, Angelina.

In the old abandoned house,
sections of ceiling hang limp in the stagnant air.
Fragments of plaster lie damp over a long untrodden floor,
their only purpose is to soak in the seasonal rain.

Cold water seeps through window frames,
rotten and blistered,
to nurse the mildew
and rise up wallpapers that peel.
All around are the artifacts
of a life lived and hastily abandoned,
mattresses, dolls, and old sepia photographs.

"The Blackened Soul" by Kirsty Cordwell

INTRODUCTION

An abandoned house is not some office building that went out of business. It once was a place where the people who lived inside shared love, tears, pain and joy. It was once full of hope, wishes, laughter and maybe even a little daydreaming. Abandoned houses always carry the weight of a sad back story. People do not just leave their beloved precious objects behind unless something terrible has happened to them. A house holds the key to so many irreplaceable memories. When you are walking into an abandoned house, you are walking into someone's time capsule. When you touch and examine the precious things that someone has left behind, it leaves you with an impression of their being. The photographs, the clothing and the toys that lay discarded when you walk through one of these houses are pieces of a puzzle to their life's story.

When visiting an abandoned home and choosing to write about it, one must handle it with care, and show consideration to those whose lives you are intruding upon. It is not something to take lightly. It is a fragile and delicate subject, not because the walls can fall apart physically, but because how it fell apart emotionally, for those that lived there once upon a time. There is something very intimate and haunting about a place that was so intensely lived in, then was suddenly left alone to wither and decay. While a home that is lived in is alive and feels warm, in an abandoned home all that is left is a cold, sad dampness of its memory lost in time. It is no longer considered an inviting presence, but instead a skeletal shell where no light ever turns on. It remains in darkness forever—until it is destroyed—then forgotten, along with the stories of those whom dwelled within.

Ingrid at Curtis Mansion, 2004.

Self portrait, 2004.

1

CAPTAIN BURKE'S CASTLE

Location: [Demolished] 4462 N Bay Road, Miami, FL

HISTORY

If you drove by the back streets of the residential area in Miami Beach in the early 2000s, a castle that looked straight out of a fairytale greeted you. It had gargoyles, mermaids, knights, wrought-iron fences, a moat complete with menacing sharks swimming inside, dragons and tall towers. It was the only house that looked completely out of place in all of Miami and it was amazing.

This house was the brainchild of a man called Captain Burke. In order to understand the fortune with which he created this house, and then the bad decisions which made him lose it, you must also understand the man and the kind of company that he built. His tumultuous life was a rollercoaster, and unfortunately, he did not have the happy fairytale ending he would have hoped for. This was a man that lived big, then lost big. He built his castle in the sand, and then the ocean came and washed it all away. For someone who had so much success, he passed away almost penniless. I am going to summarize the main points but there is so much more. There are numerous books and articles written by journalists on the events that unfolded, which can be found in the library or in book stores. He is one of the modern-day legends of Miami.

Capt. Michael Burke was born on May 13, 1924, in Bradley Beach, New Jersey. Burke was the son of Russian-Jewish immigrants. Straight out of high school, Burke served in the US Navy during World War II and spent three years on a submarine. After the war, Burke arrived in Miami Beach and began a job painting houses. That's where he met June Tuttle, his wife of fifty-seven years. The Burkes had six children, beginning with Michael Jr. in 1957, followed closely by Janeen, then Susan, Danny, Polly and finally, Joey.

Burke started a cruising company after he purchased a sailboat and renovated it. It was a 19 ft. dinghy, named *The Hangover*. He started the business because he loved to take friends to the Bahamas and they would contribute money for fuel and other necessities. He soon realized this could become a successful business, so he sold his painting company, bought a larger boat, and conceived Windjammer Barefoot Cruises. It was an enormous sacrifice at first, and they struggled to pay the bills. Acknowledged as the last authentic Caribbean pirate, Burke was faithful to his nature and wandered around his Miami Beach home with a large macaw on his shoulder. His eccentric reputation and his flamboyant disposition, made Burke a memorable personage who affected the lives of countless customers of his cruise empire.

Encyclopædia Britannica
Encyclopædia Britannica
Encyclopædia Britannica
19
18
1989
BOOK
'Clopædia Britannica
1992
BOOK
of the
YEAR
Events of
1991

O'NEILL
BY
ARTHUR AND
BARBARA GELB
Kerlinger
FOUNDATIONS OF
BEHAVIORAL
RESEARCH
IN THE COMPANY OF ELVES
A LIFE TIME
OF BEAUTY

Atlantic
THE LAST GREAT RACE OF PRINCES

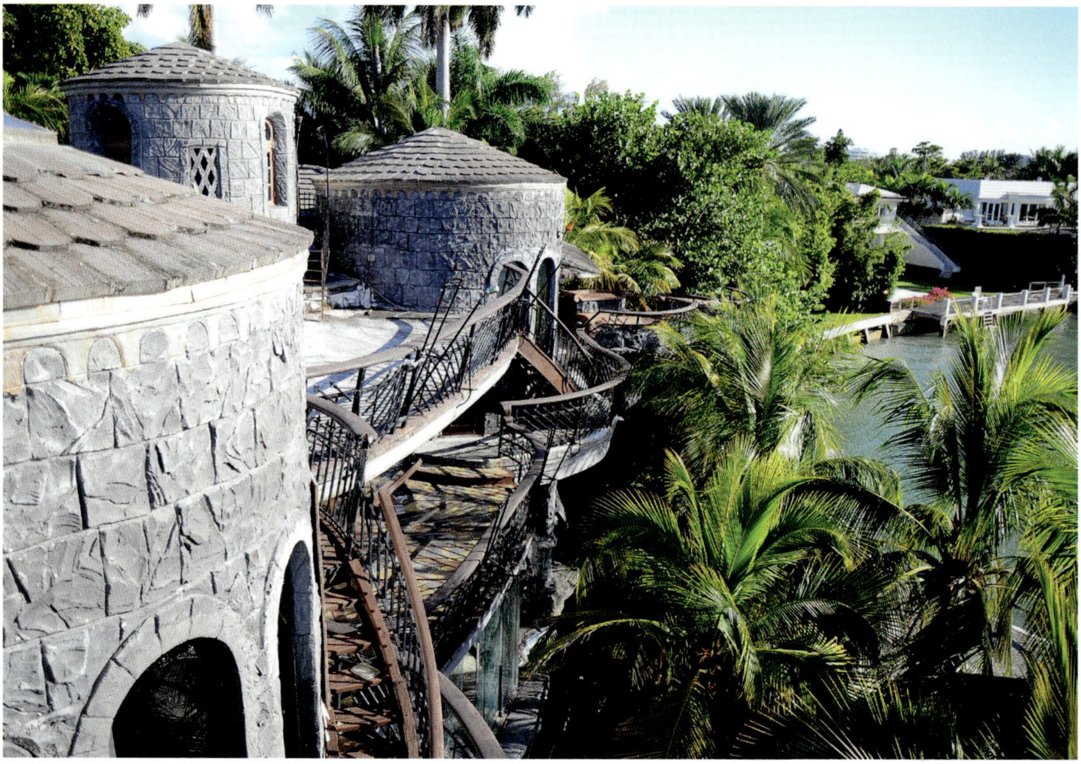

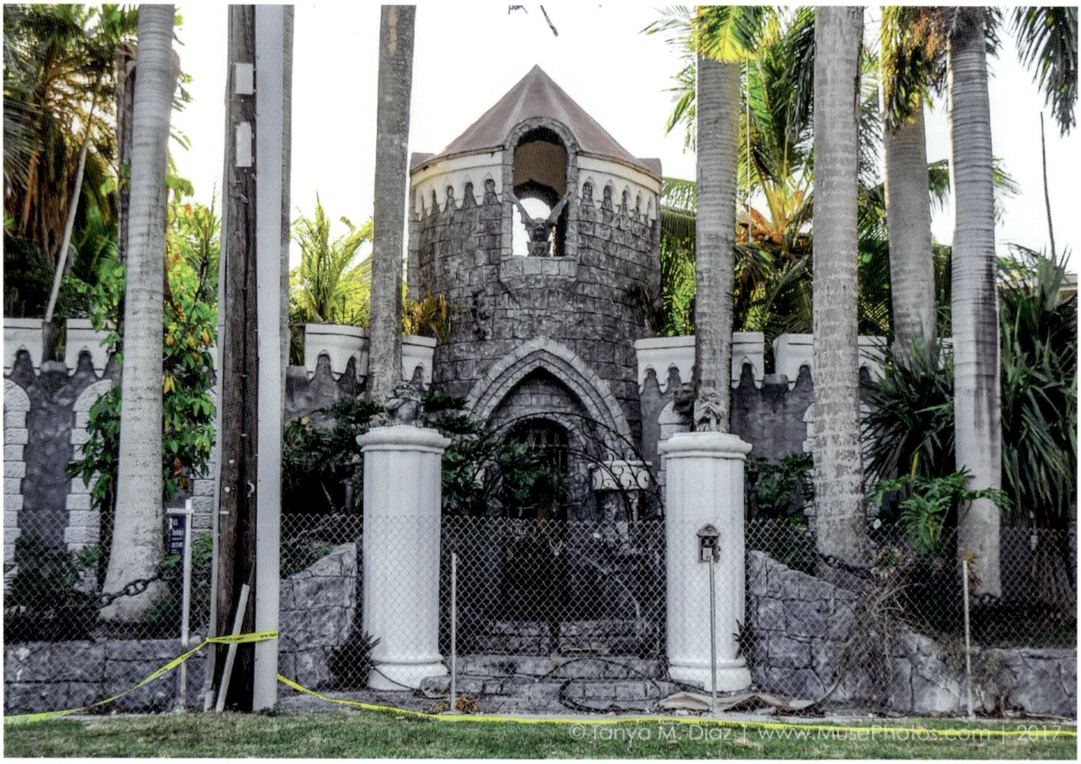
©Tanya M. Diaz | www.MusePhotos.com | 2017

Windjammer expanded and became the most extensive line of authentic tall sail ships in the world. They owned six large vessels and offered a life of partying and fun. The cruises took passengers on one or two-week trips to the Caribbean with destinations including the Bahamas, the British Virgin Islands, Costa Rica and Belize.

Windjammer Cruises was one of the first to introduce alcohol as part of the cruise fare, so they became extremely popular. They offered rum blends called swizzles at boarding and cocktail hour, cheap wine at dinner and Bloody Marys in the morning. Passengers ate, slept and drank, whenever and wherever, as much as they wanted. These were cruises where anything was allowed. Windjammer ships would sail into Caribbean island ports, raise a pirate flag and shoot blanks out of their cannons at the other cruise ships. Knowing they had the other ship passengers' full attention, the Jammers would pull down their shorts for a mass "mooning" to the vessels as they were crossing.

The number of faithful Jammers increased in the 1990s as the ships made it easy to get to know each other, and the internet made it simple to stay in touch. Many of these young people were cruising as often as they could, making statements saying that they lived and worked solely for their next Windjammer cruise in their message board called the "Coconut Telegraph." A favorite saying of the cruisers was, "What happens on a Windjammer cruise, stays on a Windjammer cruise."

The second half of the 1990s was a great success for Windjammer. With a growing family by 1995, Windjammer Cruises was on top of the world. The captain sold his house on Miami's pricey Star Island to Robert Van Winkle (a.k.a. Vanilla Ice), and bought two homes on North Bay Road. He consolidated the two properties into one colossal castle, right on Biscayne Bay in Miami Beach. No blueprints were ever used. Instead, sources claim it came right out of Burke's imagination. It was a literal manifestation of his dreams. The castle also became a magical place for his grandchildren—they were able to grow up in a world full of pirates, knights, mermaids, gargoyles and sharks.

The castle was legendary, valued at $6,000,000 when it was first built. The stunning ten bedrooms and seven bathrooms had a multitude of features, such as a dinner table styled after the knights of the roundtable. It had a 65,000-gallon seawater moat complete with shark-infested waters and a drawbridge. There were sinister looking gargoyles, sculptures of knights and dragons, men in suits of armor, a great hall complete with a chandelier to match and areas with rich, ornate, dark-wooden cabinetry. The patio had a heated, lagoon-style pool extending into the house with a twisting-serpent dragon slide. On the side of the lavish pool there was a statue of a Buddha that spouted a stream of urine out of a huge penis. It was bizarre, but that was his style.

He had parties for every occasion, and those invited would never think of not attending. Some guests even arrived by boat through the dock in the back. It was a sexually charged atmosphere full of free love, sex, drugs, and guns. The captain was known to sexually harass women, but back then he had celebrity status and he was loved, so ladies welcomed the attention from him.

The cruise line with six ships was a huge moneymaker, and the Burke's didn't feel the need to reinvest any of their money back into their company. Instead, they favored pushing the profit envelope as far as possible—even taking risks on such things as not paying for insurance, and deliberately postponing regular maintenance on their ships. This proved to be their ultimate demise.

THE FATE OF THE FANTOME

At the peak of Windjammer's popularity in 1998, the line's flagship was the *Fantome*, a beautiful 282-foot tall schooner. The prophecy of its fate ironically was in its name. In 1969, Captain Burke flew to Greece to purchase the schooner directly from its owner, Aristotle Onassis of the Onassis family, the same family as the former First Lady, and wife of John F. Kennedy, Jaqueline Onassis. He traded the *Fantome* in exchange for a freighter ship, which was a bargain, and soon the ship became the company's biggest earner—the flagship of their fleet of six vessels. She was beautiful inside and out, and was extremely popular with travelers. It's important to note though, that Captain Guyan March, the *Fantome* commodore who had spent most of his entire career working for Windjammer, once stated in an interview, that she "floated like a pig."[1]

In his daredevil pirate way, Burke took the usual careless step of electing not to buy the ship the necessary insurance. Ship premiums are extremely high, but in retrospect, as the Burke family would soon find out, it would have been worth it.

An intricately detailed account is laid out in the book, *The Ship and The Storm,* by Jim Carrier. The *Fantome* was cruising in the Western Caribbean in 1998 when tropical depression system No. 46 appeared in the southern Atlantic. Even though hurricane winds can reach 150 mph, most storms progress slower than the speed at which a cruise ship can sail, and Hurricane Mitch was at least still two days away. The *Fantome* could sail nearly twice as fast as the storm, so Burke was understandably not concerned. In a surprising move though, Hurricane Mitch sharply intensified from a tropical depression into a full-blown hurricane, and then Mitch made another unpredicted move and changed its path from the usual northwesterly arc straight west towards Cuba.

Csnavely0319. 1993. "Windjammer Barefoot Cruise Lines' SV Fantome off of Dominica". Wikipedia. January 1, 1993.

The ship landed at a port in Omoa, Honduras. There, the locals advised the captain to drop anchor and ride out the storm, but Burke back in the Miami office instructed Captain March, by telephone, to take the passengers and go to Belize City. In Belize, some non-essential crew-members disembarked with the passengers, but thirty-one staff and crew remained on board.

They only had one chance to get the trajectory right, but the predicted path for any hurricane is always an inexact science. Mitch was full of surprises, so planning where to take *Fantome* was an educated guess. They decided to consult the National Hurricane Service to see what the experts were predicting, and weigh their options.

Hurricane Mitch headed toward Swan Island as the computer models had predicted, and they also said that the storm would turn to the northwest. Expecting Mitch to stay to the north, the ship headed southeast from Belize to a small channel on the side of the Bay Islands, which is north of Honduras, hoping to take refuge. If all had gone as planned, there would have been a reasonable chance of survival, because at this point, there was still a relatively safe distance between the ship and the storm—although high seas and heavy winds were still very likely.

Mitch liked being unpredictable though, and again challenged custom when it turned directly toward the Bay Islands as a category five and destroyed everything in its path. They might as well have had a bull's eye painted on the side of the ship. The hurricane started blowing with winds and waves that extended out 200 miles from the center of the storm. Caught in a narrow channel with no place to run, Captain Guyan March had no choice but to try to weather the storm, so he steered the vessel and headed into the waves to avoid broadsides.

Captain Burke, during these last hours, kept the conversation on speakerphone; asking Captain March to keep the satellite phone open, even though Guyan could not talk much. Captain March reported waves of 35 feet and said conditions were getting worse. Visibility was almost zero. The wind and rain battered the ship every few seconds. Knowing the ship would now be facing the dirty part of the storm, Burke told March to forget the ship and save himself and the crew. Burke kept asking if the decks were clearing water, and March kept replying that they were.

The last conversation they had revealed something different:

"That was a big one," March said.

"Is it falling off, is it shedding?" Burke asked.

"Yes, that's not a prob ... "

And the line went dead.[2]

On October 27, 1998, the *Fantome*, Captain Guyan March and the thirty-one crew members onboard vanished without a trace into the sea. On November 2, a helicopter dispatched by the British destroyer HMS *Sheffield* discovered life rafts and vests, labeled "S/V *Fantome*," off the eastern coast of Guanaja. They were the only things ever found. No one survived, and a memorial service was held on December 12, 1998. Captain Burke was said to have remarked shortly after the phone went dead, "I'm going to prison for this," but he was never charged.[3]

The loss of *Fantome* plagued Captain Burke for years. He had nightmares and often said he wished he had gone down with the crew. Between the lawsuits from crew members' families, and the loss of the uninsured flagship, it made a serious dent in the company's bottom line.

By late 2005, the empire Burke had built began to crumble. Within a few years, the business became officially non-operational. Most of the Burkes had multi-million-dollar homes, bought by company money, and by then the company's accounting had become so convoluted that even Burke couldn't keep track of what they could afford. Even though the ships were falling apart, his children soon spent any little profit that was made. It is said that by the end, the captain had lost all faith in his kids, and was said to have remarked, "Go ahead and eat the company alive, and then we'll see how you feel when everything we built is gone."[4] Burke suffered a stroke that year that left him incapacitated.

Two years later in 2007, the company's president, Burke's son Daniel Burke, died of a drug overdose. The company ceased operations to mourn for several weeks. In mid-2007, they announced that they planned to relaunch the cruises on its fleet of ships, starting with S/V *Legacy* on November 3, 2007, followed by some other ships in the spring of 2008, but the S/V *Legacy* was later spotted tied up in Costa Rica in a run-down condition. Press releases in late 2007 informed the public that the company had canceled all sailings through January of 2008. They distributed no further information after 2007, and no trips were ever rescheduled. The last press release on their website is dated December 21, 2007. Windjammer Barefoot Cruises finally went bankrupt, and its remaining assets were auctioned off. Also that year, the family put the castle up for sale. In March of 2007 it sold for $7,600,000, and in January 2009 it was recorded as a foreclosure. In July of 2009, almost six months after I took my photos, the home mysteriously burned down. A week after the fire, the youngest son Joey Burke died in his sleep at forty-six. The eighty-nine-year-old Burke succumbed to pneumonia and died on May 19, 2013.[5] As of today, the lot stands empty.

MY EXPLORATIONS

I remember back in 1999, my friend Alexandra and I would always drive by every time we were on our way home from the beach. We kept hoping to catch a glimpse of the people who lived inside. Then, one day in January of 2009, the universe gave me the chance I had always dreamed of.

Another friend, Emily, joined me when I went to document it, because Alexandra couldn't make it and I didn't want to lose any precious time. We made plans to go early in the morning to have enough time to take pictures of everything. When we walked in, the side gate had no lock and was completely open. It led down a long walkway that connected to a beautiful garden. It really was like walking into a storybook. A huge shark fountain sat in the middle, full of green water. Most of the smaller statues were broken, but this one was still intact. The garden was a small maze of different little bridges with green plants on both sides. There were two small towers by the front of the garden that looked out onto the street with gargoyles perched on top. The back of the garden lead to the front door of the house which was boarded up. There was a crest embedded into the cement—it reminded me of the King Arthur stories, because it had two swords crossed over a metal helmet. Over to the side was the entrance to a grotto that led to some stairs for a pool slide that ended in a double dragon's head. The pool looked like a lazy river with little bridges and palm trees, but the water was now brown and stagnant. All the sharks that used to swim inside it were long gone.

The sliding glass doors opened easily. The inside of this house was marvelous. You could see the intricate details everywhere. It had a custom-made feel which featured little details built specifically for the owner, like the stain glass or the ornate ceilings. Even the round beds and carved wooden drawers were a part of the overall design built into the home. In the foyer, hung a huge chandelier, and beyond it, a fireplace with balconies looking over from the second floor on both sides. Encyclopedias still lined the shelf by the fireplace untouched. I didn't know the person when I was walking through, but I was puzzled as to why there were so many books on boats and the ocean. He seemed truly obsessed with nautical themes. There was a bar, a huge pool table, an aquarium that was completely empty, and a full bar next to a now-defunct TV room.

We had this strange sense of foreboding while walking through the house, even though we had no idea about the life of the man who created it. The castle seemed cursed. I later found out one of his sons had died there a year before. I got to explore every room in the castle. Any pictures, even mine, do not do it justice. It truly was a work of art—one fit for a king, or in this case, a wild pirate-captain.

2

AL CAPONE'S HOUSE

Location: 93 Palm Ave, Palm Island Miami [Currently for Sale]

A Mob Boss' Final Resting Place

The infamous house at 93 Palm Avenue, where supposedly Al Capone planned the St. Valentine's day massacre, sits on Palm Island—a man-made plot of land, created in 1919 by developer Locke Highleyman. The 30,000 sq. ft. waterfront estate is a collection of three houses: a gate house, a main villa, and a pool cabana.

In the early part of the 1920s, Miami was thriving from a boost in tourist economy, because for the first time, the middle class had the time and money to travel for leisure. Miami authorities liberalized rules for dog and horse racing, and it became extremely easy to conduct lucrative illegal business ventures.[1]

Miami also had help from developers like Carl G. Fisher, who once purchased an illuminated billboard in Times Square proclaiming "It's Always June in Miami", while bathing suit beauties basked in the sun. Soon after, Miami Beach became the most highly sought after beach resort destination in the United States.[2]

The house was built in 1922 as an investment property, by a successful, Pennsylvanian born realtor named Clarence M. Busch. Al Capone bought the house in 1928, under his wife's name. He purchased it for $40,000. The owner at the time, James W. Popham, was furious when he found out through insurance records that the realtors had happily sold the house to the infamous Chicago criminal. Popham had been lead to believe that he had been selling it to the son of a former mayor.[3] Upon discovering the truth, Popham went to court and filed a lawsuit to foreclose on the property for $30,000—saying he had sold it to a Mr. Parker Henderson, and that the Capone's had never paid any part of the debt.[3, 4]

Florida Governor Doyle Carlton also had it out for him, and told every leader in every county to do whatever they could to prevent the gangster's move to the magic city. They tried to make his life a waking nightmare and he was arrested multiple times.[5] The City of Miami stated Capone's home was "a menace to the safety and well-being of residents."[6]

Capone had made quite a name for himself. In 1925, he became notoriously infamous and had risen to the ranks of supreme gangster boss in the crime syndicates of Chicago. Newspapers from all over the world were talking about him. Hollywood movies painted the mob king as a ruthless and blood-thirsty murderer, so the people of Miami were understandably upset with the idea of Capone being a neighbor.

In spite of the odds though, Capone was determined to stay and make Palm Island his paradise. He spent $200,000 creating a winter command post with a gate, a guest house, a 7-ft. high wall, search lights, a cabana and a coral rock grotto. Miamians eventually started warming up to the idea of him after they were able to enjoy the wealth and generosity he was injecting into the depressed economy. To further clean up his image, he invited several reporters to his famous spaghetti and steak parties. Even though he was known for turning bootlegging into a lucrative business during the Prohibition era, he kept a responsible image on these occasions by making sure no alcohol was served. Yet people still felt he was a danger and going to cause gang fights because neighbors saw and heard the all-night parties, orgies and even occasional gunfire.

In 1931, his good image with the city ran out and Capone was arrested by the federal government for tax evasion. He was sent to the maximum-security prison, Alcatraz, for eleven years. In the end, he only completed eight years of the sentence, because he started showing signs of early onset dementia after the rough conditions in the prison traumatized him. He was able to return to the Florida mansion, but his condition worsened, and his mind eventually regressed to that of a twelve-year-old. He spent his final days in a room above the front entrance driveway where he could keep an eye on who came and went. After suffering a bad stroke after a harsh long battle with pneumonia, his heart failed on January 25, 1947, at the age of forty-eight. He died peacefully in bed, surrounded by family.[7]

Capone's personal bathroom in 2005.

THE CAPONE FAMILY CURSE

The last surviving family member born with the name Capone was his niece Deirdre, who was one of the few who actually knew the original man once known as "Scarface". Sharing her last name with the man who was once America's most feared criminal was very similar to having a lifelong curse. Being a Capone has been an extremely traumatic experience for her. When she was only ten years old, her father committed suicide after reading a manuscript written about their family. She was also fired from her first full-time job when her employer discovered who she was. She quickly learned to hide her name because she feared what people would think of her. She didn't even tell her children who she really was until they were older.[8]

Left: The room where Al Capone died in 2005.

Below: Al Capone (no copyright)

After Capone's death, the house at 93 Palm Avenue went through numerous quick sales. Not one owner ever remained in possession of the property for a substantial amount of time. It has had eleven owners in sixty-seven years. That's an average of six years per owner. In 1952, Mae Capone, Al Capone's wife, sold the house to Cleveland realtor Thomas Warren Miller, who later sold it to Mr. Harry Renckert four years later in 1956. Then he sold it in 1959 to Laurence Marcus. Next it was sold to Dr. James C. Chimerakis, a Coral Gables physician and surgeon in 1960. In October 1967, Dr. Chimerakis tried to sell the house for $75,000, but it remained on the market until it finally sold to William Knowles on June 12, 1968, for $48,000. In 1969, he sold it to Mr. Roy Fowler for $50,000. A few years later, in 1971, Delta airline pilot Henry T. Morrison purchased the mansion for $56,000 and didn't know it was once owned by Al Capone. Ironically, he was the longest standing owner. At a total of forty years, he lived there longer than Capone himself, who only owned it for a total of nineteen years. Morrison remodeled it in 1982, and he lived there until he placed the house on the market. For almost five years from 2006 until 2011, it remained unsold until Peter L. Corsell, founder of the smart energy company Grid Point, bought it for $5.7 million.[9] He renovated the house and quickly sold it two years later in 2013 to an anonymous French couple. Then it was sold again a year later in May 2014, when MB America purchased the home for 8 million and renamed it 93 Palm. In March 2015, after a complete $1.4-million refurbishment, it was opened as an exclusive production venue which rented itself out to anyone who could pay the high price to use the mansion as a photo and video shooting location. It must not have been very lucrative for MB because the ninety-three-year-old historic home was sold to European soccer agent Mino Riaola for $9 million in August of 2016, but the home is currently for sale once again two years later for $13,500,000.[10]

The house seems extremely problematic and news articles in years past have joked about the various owners. The quick sales have earned the house the title of the Capone Curse. It would seem anything associated with Capone gives the opposite effect of turning things to gold. Could this be true or has the bloody history of Al Capone caused buyers to have a change of heart after the sale? What would make so many owners quickly sell such a beautiful house? While its dark historical past might be the most logical explanation, there also may be something more.

When I went in 2007, I was personally told by the realtors who hired me to take the pictures that there had been numerous paranormal occurrences in the house. They didn't go into too many details, but did state that many of the lights turn off and on, doors open and close by themselves, and there are sounds of people talking when no one is there. Of course, there have been several appearances by Capone himself—who I was told wanders around upstairs, close to the room where he passed away, and through the vast gardens. I was told to keep the story quiet until they sold it because they didn't want to ruin the sale. They never sold the house though, because that privilege went to a different realtor team who sold it to MB in 2011.[11]

A house this old is sure to have some strong energies creeping around. I don't doubt for a second that there is something there, but I didn't spend enough time in the house to experience any activity. The feeling of the house inside seemed dark and strange. Besides knowing the former history, the way it was decorated also lended itself to the feeling of an unkempt abandoned house. The color of the walls and the furniture when I took the photos were vastly different from the cheery, bright sophisticated photos you can find of it on the internet today. When the realtors led me through the house and pointed out the room that Capone died in, I instantly felt shivers crawl up my spine. I was left to wander around alone and take whatever pictures I could, but I wanted to get out of there as soon as possible. While my pictures are not as pretty as the ones taken by other photographers after it was remodeled, they do show a dimension of the house that more closely resembles its original look.

3

THE REDLINGER ORCHIDS ORNAMENTAL NURSERY

Location: [Demolished] 9236 SW 57th Ave Miami, FL 33156

THE FASCINATING FLOWER FARM

The Redlinger Orchids Ornamental Nursery was an orchid farm that opened in the 1960s, located in Pinecrest, Florida. It was the business of Joseph Richard Redlinger, who became very successful and gained international notoriety for his original orchid crosses. He is most known for a cross breed he created in 1981, known as the Phalaenopsis Misty Green. He was born in Luxembourg, Germany, in 1919, and had both Jewish Ashkenazi and German roots. When he first arrived in America, he lived in Mobile, Alabama, but not much else is known of his early life. His family in Miami stated that he did not keep any written records of that time, but it is known that in his early life he was in the military. He was married twice, once to a woman named Jean, and had two children. Later in life, he married Ana Redlinger, who is one of the sweetest and most interesting women I have ever met. They had two children, Linda and Joseph Redlinger III. His son is a personal friend of mine. Joseph Richard Redlinger II passed away in his beautiful orchid farm surrounded by his family in 1999. I met his son many years later in 2010.

ORCHIDS

OPEN

Joseph bought the empty plot of land when that area of Miami had just started development. The first part of the house was built in 1955 and it was the first house on that road. He made it to his specifications. He wanted it to be his home and to be able to have his orchid laboratory and nursery business. Unfortunately, when the area started getting populated, many of his neighbors complained that he was doing illegal business in a residential area. For weeks he battled with the Metro Zoning Board and it seemed as if everything would be lost, because at first they voted against him. He kept appealing the decision. I found an article where it stated he would just keep coming right back to try and convince them—every time they said no. This went on for twenty-two months and apparently he was so persistent that he finally did convince them, and they voted for him to keep his beautiful orchid nursery in his residential home.[1]

Over the years, he made a few additions to the house. He built a pool and some extra rooms after his children were born. After he passed away, Ana tried to hold onto the business as long as she could, but after so many years it was just too big to maintain. No one was breeding the orchids anymore. She sold the house in June of 2015 for $949,000 and moved to a smaller place with her son. She told me that the house has had several owners after they moved, but no one would stay for very long. The house was demolished and sold to a man that had trouble with the city regarding the permits to rebuild on the land. Then he sold it and the house was demolished. In the lot, the new owners built a modern-looking box house. It is very pretty, but it has none of that wild overgrown charm of the former one. It is currently on sale for $6,475,000.

Photo courtesy of Joseph Redlinger III.

My Explorations

The first time I saw the Redlinger Orchid Nursery, I went with my friend Emily to do a photoshoot. She had been telling me about this guy she was dating who lived in a magical house in Pinecrest. She wanted me to take pictures of her in its lush, overgrown yard. She also kept telling me that I had to meet his mom, Ana, because she was so nice. When I arrived at the house, it all suddenly jogged my memory. I recognized it right away and knew very well who this man was. For years I used to drive by 57th Avenue to go to my other friend's house, and I would always see Joseph out in front of his home selling orchids. I actually bought one from him, and I remembered his face. I had asked him to pick a nice one for my mom on Mother's Day. I later found out that was only a few years before he died. The world is so small sometimes. We did our shoot and we talked for the longest time with Ana. I remember leaving and thinking I really wanted to keep in touch with her. Her energy inside and out was so alive and beautiful! I never did go back, and then shortly after, Joseph and Emily stopped dating. I really didn't think I would ever see them, or the house again.

One day, I asked my daughter if she wanted to go for a bike ride. Pinecrest is a very lush, expensive suburban area on the outskirts of the city. It has tons of huge old oak trees, beautiful mansions and great sidewalks for running and riding bikes. On the way there, I didn't notice the house, nor did I even remember it existed. On my way back though, I was riding along and I suddenly stopped in my tracks. There on my left was the house with its gates completely open, and it looked totally abandoned. I walked inside to see if Ana or Joseph were around, but everything was deserted. My daughter and I walked around a bit, but the sun was getting very low, and we were still very far from where I had parked the car. I took down the address and sent Emily a text fearing the worst. I thought Ana had died. She was able to get a hold of his sister who told her that she was alive and kicking. They just sold the house because it was too much for her to maintain alone.

I went back about three times afterward—once doing an amazing photoshoot of myself, then a few other times with friends. I loved walking around and finding new things. Once, I found old bottles of chemicals he used to make the formulas to feed the orchids. I always felt safe and at peace there. Ana says it's because his spirit liked my energy.

When I was writing this book, I was able to talk to Ana for a while. She told me all about their lives and her time in the house, how she was from Costa Rica and how she had married Joseph when he was older. She said he was a great father to all his children. She told me about the additions they had made and about the age of the original house. Then, as if telling me a big secret, she said in a hushed tone, "But you know, there are spirits in that house." She says she isn't sure if it was Joseph teasing her or not, but he had told her the house had been part of a much bigger plot of land that had been a Native American Indian burial ground. Over the years, she had very strange experiences; hearing her name being called when there was no one there or seeing apparitions. Ana said the strangest thing that ever happened was one night while they were all eating dinner, the French doors to the pool area shook so hard she thought they were going to burst out of their frames. She said Joseph had never believed in spirits and had dismissed it as just some plane flying overhead, but no one actually heard the plane—on that occasion or the few others that followed. Then, after a few years, it just never happened again. I knew about the spirits from years before, because when Emily was dating Joseph, she had also heard her name being called a few times. She would also get strange nightmares when she would sleep over. Apparently, it was something that happened to everyone if you hung around there long enough. I honestly never saw or heard anything, but I always felt like I was being watched, even though no one was there. We have all agreed though, if it was a spirit or many spirits, none of them were ever malicious. The energy there wasn't dark or evil—on the contrary, it was an abandoned place full of light and peace. I am so happy I got to experience and photograph it so extensively before it was demolished. I am hoping to keep Joseph Richard Redlinger and his beautiful Orchid farm as part of Miami's permanent history. He was a true legendary botanist, and a wonderful father and husband who was very loved, and is missed by all those that knew him.

Hopefully this tribute will help those in Miami remember the old man that used to sell the amazing orchids by the side of the road for so many years. This way, the story of his beautiful nursery, that he fought so hard to keep, will live on forever.

Photo courtesy of Joseph Redlinger III.

Photo courtesy of Joseph Redlinger III.

Photo courtesy of Joseph Redlinger III.

Photo courtesy of Joseph Redlinger III.

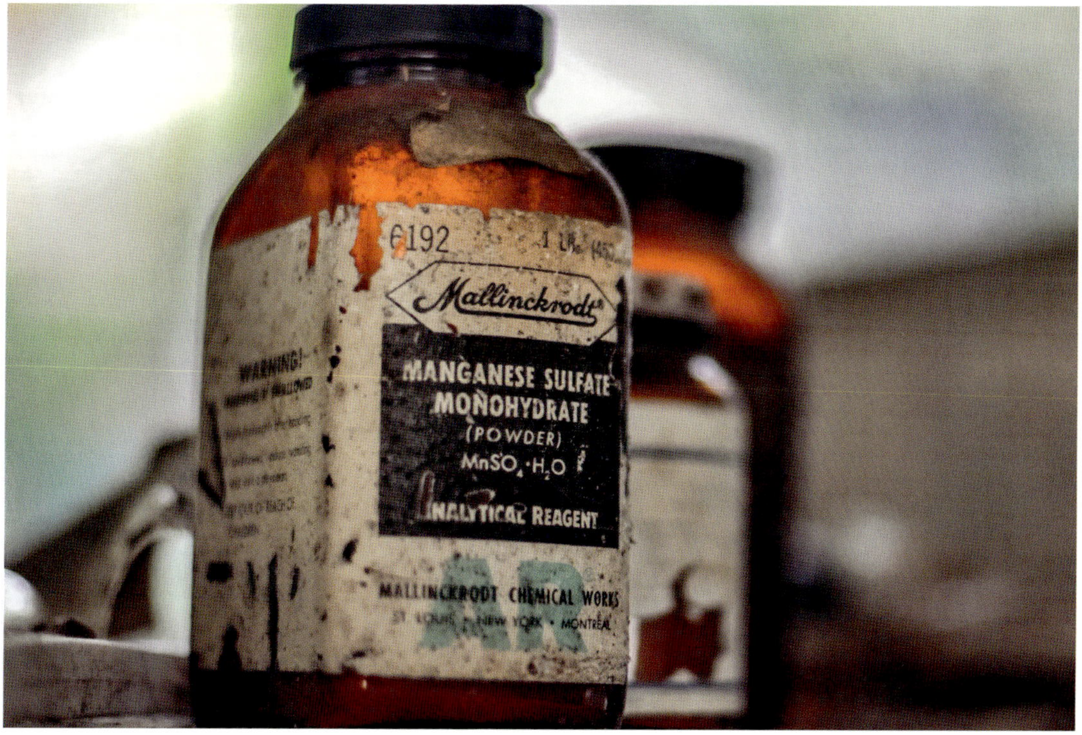

6192
Mallinckrodt
MANGANESE SULFATE
MONOHYDRATE
(POWDER)
MnSO$_4$·H$_2$O
ANALYTICAL REAGENT
MALLINCKRODT CHEMICAL WORKS
ST. LOUIS · NEW YORK · MONTREAL
WARNING!

500 ml
PYREX
USA
No. 4980
STOPPER No. 7

Photo courtesy of Joseph Redlinger III.

Photo courtesy of Joseph Redlinger III.

Above: Self-portrait taken at the Orchid Farm.

Right: Photo by Munna Rangam.

Photo by Lissette Ibis Velez-Cuniberti.

Photo by Munna Rangam.

Lissette Ibis Velez-Cuniberti at the Orchid Farm.

Emily Swiatek at the Orchid Farm Pool.

Eddy De La Peña in the back with the sunglasses, Munna Rangam, and me.

4

BOCA MURDER HOUSE

Location: [Demolished] 7450 Lyons Road, Pompano Beach, Fl. 33073

The Boca House Urban Legend

Only grass remains in the empty plot of land where once stood a house that was entangled in dark horrific rumors. This house had been a puzzling mystery for my friend and I for many years. It took us a long time to track down its location, because we had been there only one time. On Saturday, around ten years ago, I drove in circles for hours trying to retrace my steps until I almost ran out of gas. After fifteen years, persistence finally paid off. I found the hard proof I needed.

While you are reading this, I want you to understand that I wrote the part of my personal experience before I actually solved the mystery of this house. Up until two days ago, it had been an elusive ghost to me. I had no idea if the story I was told fifteen years ago was real or not. I could have rewritten that part to reflect this new information, but I decided against it because I want to put you where I was for the past fifteen years. I have never been as disturbed about a rumor of a location as I was about this house. For that simple reason, this house stands apart from all the rest. I'm going to start this story opposite to all of the others and start with my story, because my personal experience was much stranger and more extraordinary than the actual history.

My Explorations

In August of 2004, I got a late-night message from a stranger on Myspace. I can't remember his name, because I blocked the guy after our first meeting, and in 2009, I deleted the Myspace profile altogether—so bear with me. We will call this

guy Myspace Man, which I personally think has a nice ring to it, don't you? So, Myspace Man told me he saw my website abandonedmuse.com, and decided to reach out to tell me about a scary looking house in Boca Raton, which had been abandoned for many years. He insisted I go photograph it. He then proceeded to tell me the most horrific backstory of any place I have ever explored.

He said the house had originally been built as a church, but one day the church had burned down. The building had been repaired and made into a house, but the family that moved in had died in a terrible murder, which had been all over the news. He said they were a Jewish couple who had two daughters. Not long after they moved in, they had marital problems and the wife started having an affair with another man. The husband found out about this and got extremely upset. One night, when she had not come home because she was away with her lover, in a frightening fit of rage, he decided to destroy her. He convinced his daughters individually to come to the bathroom. Then, one by one, he drowned them in the bathtub. He then got a shotgun, sat on his bed and blew off his head. The next day when the wife arrived, she saw what had happened and lost her mind. She was placed in a psychiatric hospital and has never recovered. A few years later, another church nearby bought the home to make it a church again. A few months after, the church had to abandon the idea because it was too haunted with demonic forces. It had been abandoned for years at that point, and I was told the girls' toys and items from the family were still inside.

I was so creeped out because it was such a disturbing story, but I thought it would be important to document its history. I was intrigued. I had never been in a place where anyone had been murdered. I wasn't sure if I wanted to go though, because I didn't want any demons (if such things exist) attaching themselves to me. I called a new friend Mike, which I had also met online. We had already hung out a few times in person. He is more of a skeptic than I am, and he told me not to worry and that he would come because there was nothing there. Myspace Man had said he usually went at night, but there was no way I was going to go to this place at night. I made plans with Mike for later that week during the middle of the day instead.

The city of Boca Raton is about forty-five minutes away from my house in Miami, so there was plenty of time for us to talk theories and speculate about the murder. The ride over was fun and I was almost feeling better—that is, until we laid eyes on the exterior of this house. I had no idea what was in there, but looking at this place made me feel pure terror. I don't get scared easily, but I had never seen a house that made me feel so uncomfortable. I commented to Mike that it looked exactly like the Amityville House, but in a South Florida style. Even the shape of the roof was eerily similar. It also had a creepy repurposed church look. The entrance to the house had two large wooden double doors with iron hinges, which made it look medieval and imposing.

We checked the door, but there was no way to get inside. Myspace Man had commented that the back was usually open. We walked around to the back and found a huge piece of plywood that was covering the back door. Someone had been there before us, and had done the job of prying the boards away from the sides, which created an opening just big enough for us to crawl inside.

Immediately upon entering the house, we both felt a strong dark presence. I don't know what it was, but it felt evil. We came in through the back of the house, so it was really dark, because all the windows in this area were closed with plywood. I took a flashlight to see what all the boxes were around me. I turned it on and immediately I froze. It was boxes and boxes of old, used toys. Mike came behind me to look and we both just stood there in silence, frozen in the dark. We were both in shock. Seeing those toys made it seem all the more real. I didn't want to touch any of it. I usually love looking at old toys, but thinking about those poor little girls made me sick. I just couldn't bring myself to look through their things.

I felt this was way over my head. It was a lot to take in. My head was racing with the possibility that a family had truly been murdered in that house. Two poor little girls died! My heart was in pieces. I wasn't sure I wanted to stay anymore. I started trying to prepare myself just in case I found something really horrible, like blood or even worse—brain matter splattered on the walls. I honestly didn't know what to expect anymore.

We had just been there five minutes, but the darkness of this place and its story was choking me. A heavy weight bore down on my chest and lungs that made it difficult for me to breathe. I was drowning in a room full of air. My mind kept screaming, "Someone died in this house! Two little girls died inside this house!" Mike says I was actually saying that out loud, but I honestly don't remember it that way.

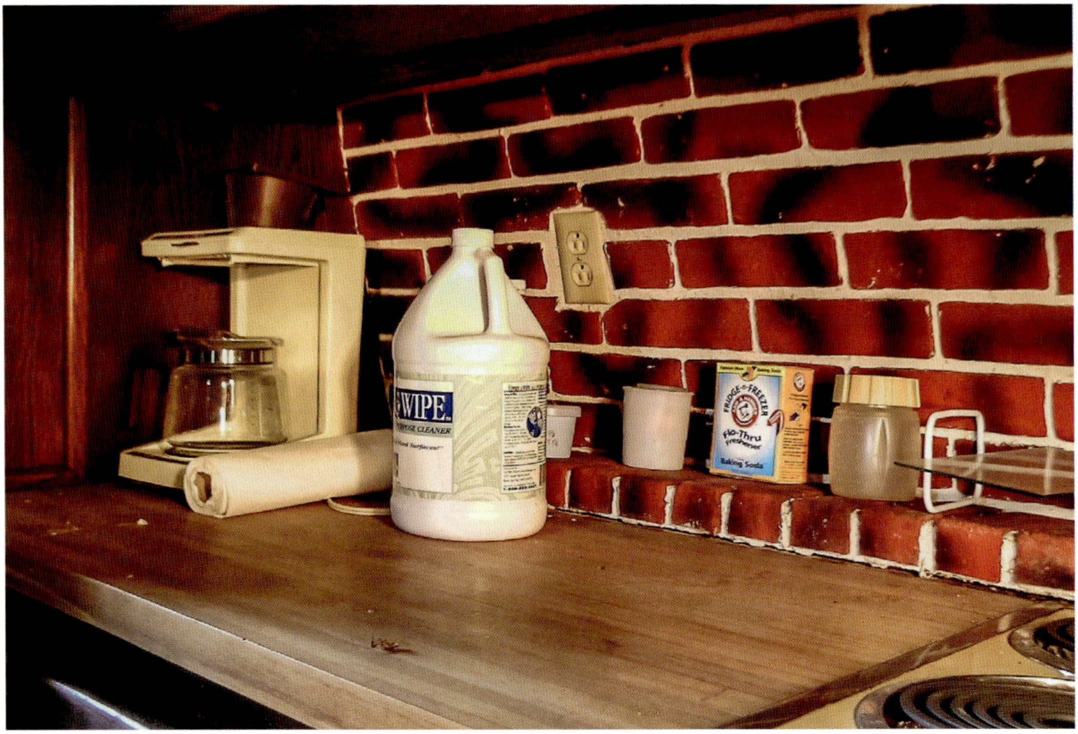
WIPE
Flo-Thru
Freshener
Baking Soda

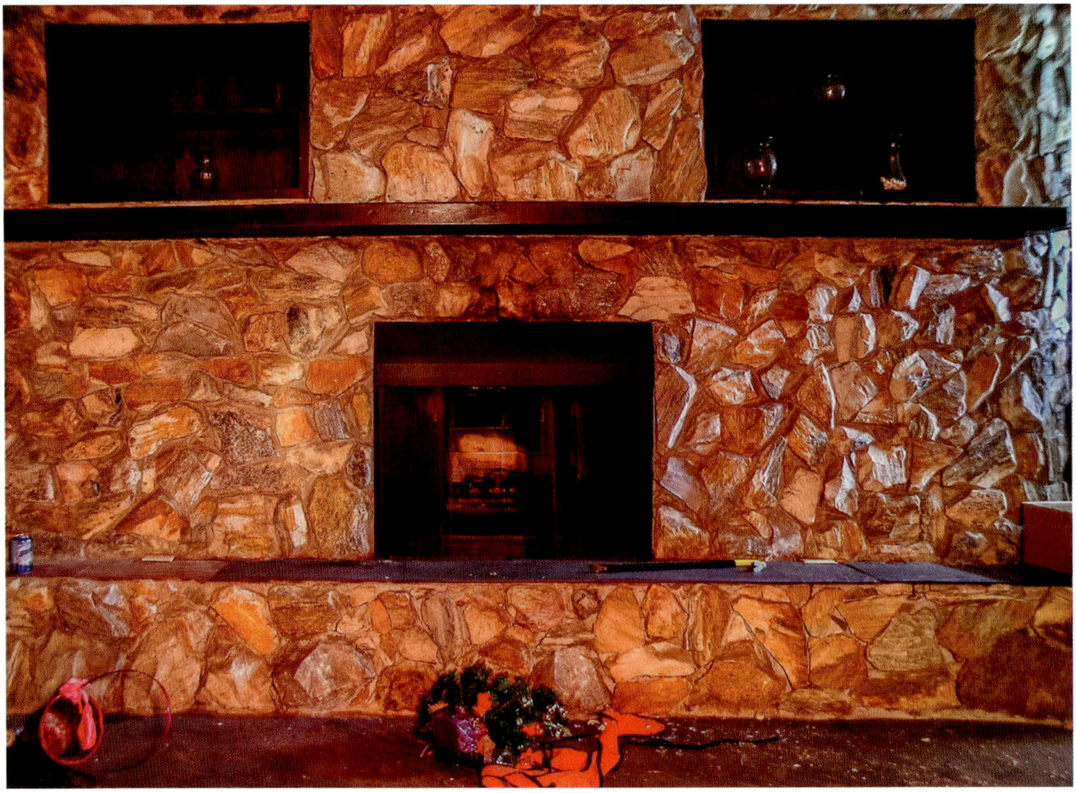

There was also this crazy, intense heat inside the house, because it was summer, and all the windows were closed. I think Mike could feel I was not okay, because he suddenly grabbed me and hugged me tight. I knew right there and then that I was never coming back to the house nor would I ever dare go into a place where something so evil had occurred.

We started walking further in, making our way toward the front of the house. There, we found boxes full of more broken toys, and also clothes, shoes and a few select pieces of furniture like chairs and sofas. The furniture also had boxes stacked on top with haphazardly placed random objects. In the huge family room fireplace, there were holiday decorations by the floor as if they were once hanging. The holiday cheer felt so out of place. The scene looked like someone had been packing up to move around the holidays and something happened, so they abandoned it all. There was a coffee maker on the kitchen counter and the clock on the oven still gave away the house's time of death—11:28.

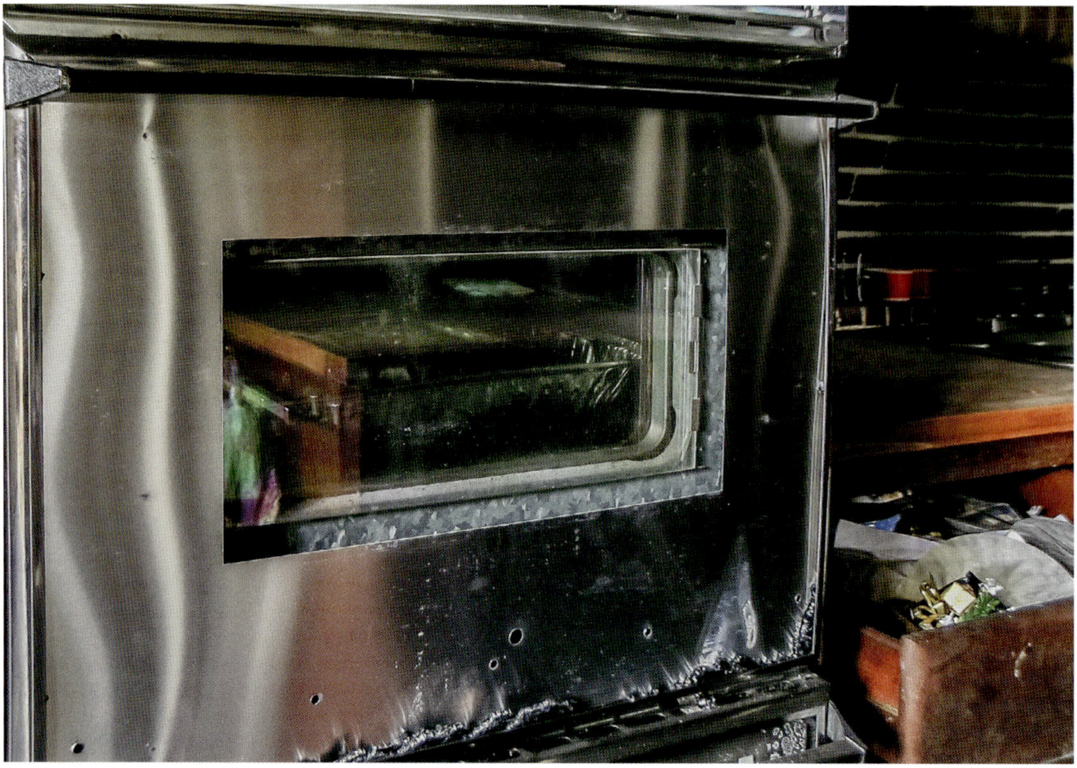

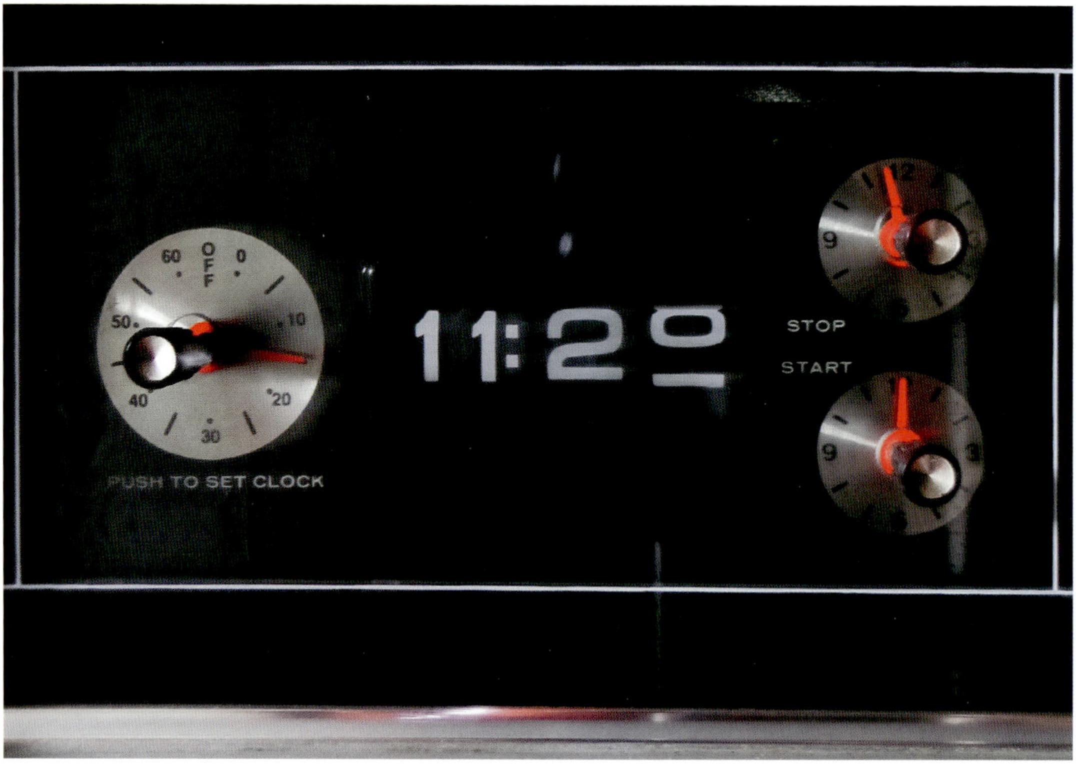

60 OFF 0
50
10
40
20
30
PUSH TO SET CLOCK
11:2
STOP
START
12
9
9

We kept looking, and in one of the mirrors there was a large crack, as if someone had punched it in anger. It also had some white milky substance that someone had splashed all over it. The kitchen drawers still had things inside, just like you would find in any regular home: ketchup packets, plastic silverware, batteries, pens, notes, tape. There was even an old remote control, but no TV—it was probably stolen long ago. We also found a piano and an organ which probably belonged to the congregation that owned the storage. While rummaging through boxes closer to the entrance, we found numerous girls' toys, a diary, and a Bat Mitzvah album. It all led us to believe the story was true. Myspace Man said the former family was Jewish and the church that bought it after was Christian.

I went upstairs alone while Mike stayed rummaging through the downstairs. Because I knew people had died there, I brought sage with me, and I lit it as I was walking around. It's an old practice used by many Native American tribes to ward off evil spirits. I spoke into the air thinking that if that man who had killed himself and his children was still there somewhere, hopefully he could hear me. I tried to send him love and forgiveness. I wanted to free him from whatever hell he had made for himself. It also helped me cope in my own way with the whole story.

I walked over to the children's bathroom, which was wall papered in bright and sunshiny hues of orange, yellow and green, but I couldn't bear to look inside that tub. I didn't even want to know what it looked like. I took pictures of the walls and light fixtures instead.

Then, as I was standing in the hallway about to go into one of the children's rooms, I heard the sound of the piano downstairs. The melody floated up and echoed all over the vaulted ceiling to reach me. Mike is an amazing multi-talented musician who plays the piano and the upright bass. He made that untuned piano sound beautiful. He played the song "Like Spinning Plates" by Radiohead. (The forward version though, not the one that goes in reverse.) I forgot about the world after that, and just closed my eyes and stood there in awe listening to every note he played. It was magical listening to that song in an abandoned house. It is a haunting melody all on its own, but being there, in that house, with him playing it made it one of the most hauntingly beautiful memories of my life.

Mike E. playing the piano.

A bit later on, I heard a noise. Mike heard it too. The wooden plank was being pulled open. Our first reaction was that the cops had found us and we rushed to hide, but then I heard someone shout my nickname, "Hey Muse, are you still here?" Mike and I looked at each other and right away I knew who it had to be. The Myspace Man had showed up with all of his friends to give us a very unwanted grand tour of the place. I had told him what day we were going but I hadn't been expecting him. He caught us off-guard and completely broke the magic spell we had together. We met him downstairs and I started to faintly feel that suffocating feeling again. We all talked for a bit downstairs and they told us a few stories about how they usually hung out there at night and would drink and smoke without the cops bothering them. Myspace Man was nice, but he had a creepy tweaker junkie vibe. His friends were pretty disrespectful, loud and obnoxious. They started rummaging through boxes and making jokes. I felt really uncomfortable there with them. I could tell Mike was annoyed too, because he was really quiet. We didn't hang around very long after that. I never got to take all the pictures I wanted, because I never went back.

Mystery Solved Fifteen Years Later

Disclaimer: I'm going to be really honest now. This part is going to get boring and completely uninteresting—so you can just skip it if you want. Don't keep reading this part if you prefer creepy stories better than plain old boring facts. I'm being serious. I kind of wish I never would have found the truth. I was sort of annoyed and disappointed with how lame the history of this place turned out to be. The next chapter is better. You can just turn the page, and nobody will know. It will be our secret. You have my total permission. Okay? Cool, see you in the next section.

Oh, wait, you said no? You would rather know the absolute truth and learn about how I went about finding it? Well then, I guess you are as nerdy as me about the facts. Let's dig in.

We had been trying since day one to find anything stating that there was a definitive murder at this house. Mike was way more skeptical than I was about the demons or ghosts, but he had been pretty spooked about the actual story. He researched it with me to find out if it was true. The day we went there, he had the idea to call around to the churches on the street in front of the house. He had taken down the number on one of their billboards and called a bunch of times, but no one ever answered. He also went to the phonebook and called places close by, but no one knew anything. Meanwhile, I called all the local newspapers and news stations in the area, yet no one had ever heard of a murder. The search kept coming up empty for both of us time and time again. We then forgot about it for a while after he moved away. Every few years though, we would reconnect. We would be sitting and talking on the phone, or we'd see each other and one of us would bring it up, so we would try to look again. We both knew if it was true, eventually one of us would find the indisputable evidence.

Over time, Mike lost the paper with the address on a move to Boston and neither one of us remembered anything more than the words Lyons Road. I also lived pretty far away, so it wasn't a place I could just drive by very often, or visit on a whim. Back until just a few years ago, the resources available for doing really extensive online research on the history of an obscure house such as this one were scarce. It would have required me to drive up to Broward to look through boxes and boxes of historical news and building archives for hours at a time. I personally didn't have that kind of time on my hands.

Now fifteen years later while writing this book, I felt that old spark of determination in me again to investigate it as far as I could. Life is more digital these days and I now know about several archives that didn't exist back then. I tried once and for all to put the whole story to rest. Mike is doing his medical residency up in Georgia right now, so I was on my own for the most part. He did go on break one day and came back with a screen shot from Google Earth giving me the the general vicinity which he remembered, but neither one of us could find that very distinctive roof the house had. I honestly had almost given up, and was already settled on the fact I was never going to find it. I had prepared my chapter with the intent that I would have to live with the fact that I was only going to be able to include my own personal account, without any of the history. Then it occurred to me to post the photo of the front of the house on Facebook and Reddit. I posted it on several Boca Raton historical groups. Days went by, though, and nothing. Just a few curious people and one guy that promised to ask a judge who was his friend, but he never got back to me. Then in a desperate last hope effort, I posted it on my newsfeed on my personal Facebook. I thought maybe someone would know someone else in the area. In any case, it was worth a shot. I had already written my chapter either way. At first, no one even bothered liking the photo—I wasn't even mad—it is a pretty ugly house. I had gone to bed disappointed. Out of nowhere, the next day around 4 PM, when I had lost every single shred of hope, my friend Brett commented that he had gone to school in that neighborhood when he was younger and would pass by that exact house every day. The irony of the whole thing, is that Brett is one of the only urban explorers on my friends list. He has invited me to quite a few places over the years. You'll hear more about him in book three. He confirmed he had heard a rumor about a murder there and sent me a screen shot of Google Earth with the exact coordinates of where it used to stand. From there, I was finally able to retrieve the correct address that we had lost so many years ago and I was able to confirm it on an old Google satellite photo. We had been searching in the right spot, but had overlooked it a dozen times because it was just an empty lot now. That was only step one. At least now I knew for certain that it had been demolished, which answered why we couldn't identify it before. Now to move onto to step two: finding the owners.

I tried cross referencing the address, but all I got were pictures of the empty lot and the price for sale. I searched the property appraiser site with the address; there I found two names, the name of a man with the last name Sanzone, and the name of a church, Primera Iglesia Bautista Hispana of Boca Raton. I looked for a murder by a person named Sanzone or the man who bought it for the congregation, but nothing appeared.

The City of Broward County digital public records start in 1974. This house was built in 1970, but I couldn't see who built it. That left a gaping hole of four years where a murder could have happened. So I had to keep digging. I called the property appraisers office and they said that they had those dates stored in boxes in a warehouse off-site— I needed to find it a different way. I looked through newspaper archives searching the address and the names I had with the word "murder"—no dice.

Finally, I did a cross search of the address, with the name Sanzone, and the name of the church. A document from a zoning case and several articles pulled up on Google. BINGO!

I was able to find other court documents that confirmed that 7450 Lyons Road was built in 1970 by the same man, Jerome Sanzone, and his wife, Carol Sanzone. I also found that Jerome was a city building code inspector for the city of Broward County. Jerome held on to the property at Lyons Road until he sold it in 1997 to the Baptist church congregation for $240,000. The church was a Hispanic Baptist institution, which was affiliated with the Southern Baptist Convention. They served a growing population of parishioners of Hispanic descent in Northern Broward County, Florida.[1]

So, what really happened? Well, it's not as interesting, but still a bit strange. The reason the property was abandoned was because the Pastor, A. Pratt closed on the sale a few months after the county had passed a zoning rule that churches within the agricultural estate zoning district must be at least 1,000 feet from other nonresidential buildings.[2] The city refused to budge, and he refused to make the property a residential home. It was abandoned on a stalemate. I told you it was disappointing. The city even stalked him to to see if he was still holding church services or small garage sales, so they could fine him (that is where those boxes with all the toys came from). The church then filed a federal court suit against Broward County over the zoning rules, which many parishioners said were arbitrarily enforced and denied them their right to religious assembly.

In another article from a local newspaper, he talked about the fact that a lot of neighbors in that area were white, upper-middle-class Americans that were not too enthusiastic about having a bunch of Hispanic people praying in their neighborhood. He stated that residents had personally come up to him to let him know they did not want any Cubans residing in the area. I was slightly offended, because my family is Cuban. I have no idea what Cubans as a whole did to these people to call us all out by name. He tried to convince the neighbors that there were only 3 Cuban families in the group and the rest were from many other diverse Latin American countries. [3] This information did not appease the xenophobic residents or the city. Low-key racism? Yes, clearly it was. He even tried to appease them and demolished the weird creepy house to build a better place, and they still wouldn't budge.

They refused to change or make an exception to the law they had just created. They had changed it less than a few months before. You can tell they were just bullies. The pastor though, played the fool's hand. Personally, I would have sold the property and bought another place somewhere else far from those people. It was apparently clear to everyone except this pastor that he wasn't going to get his way, yet he pressed on. He said he knew he would win because he had God on his side. He must have confused the words debt and God, because he spent tons of money fighting a legal battle with the city that he lost really badly. In the documents, you can see just how rude these people were to him. That's probably the bad energy I was feeling the whole time there. Those people were so shady they could bring a total eclipse in full sun.

I actually feel bad for him after reading all the court documents, because he bought the location and was informed he could build his church. Sanzone had been a building inspector for many years, so he thought he knew it all, yet didn't try and confirm the new building codes that had changed during the sale. He gave the pastor all outdated information—so it wasn't even the pastor's fault, it was Sanzone's. Despite the commission knowing it was not his fault, they still upheld the new law. They didn't show an ounce of mercy for him. Pratt bought that house for $240,000 in 1997, which is pretty big money, even in today's housing market. Twenty-two years later, he still hasn't recuperated a penny that he spent. The way I see it, it was a simple rule they had just written. They could have let it slide, considering he had just closed on the place when they signed the stupid code into law. It wouldn't have hurt any one for him to have built a church there. I'm not a fan of Baptists or churches, but fair is fair. His property could have been "grandfathered" in.

Real estate websites still show his name on the Broward County property appraiser website. All the real estate sites show a picture of a dark sky above an empty lot, *sans* the Amityville lookalike house. It is currently on sale for a whopping $300,000. It is a pricey sales tag for just a few trees and some badly mowed grass, but I imagine he is just trying to make his money back.

In the end, there was never any murder or any reason to feel any fear except for maybe some sketchy neighbors. It seems like Myspace Man might have been trying to trick me so I could go out there for whatever sinister or benign reason he may have been dreaming up. He probably thought I would go alone, but I always take someone with me. I blocked him when I got home that day, because something about him seemed off. It is also very possible he believed the whole urban legend, and was just as impressionable as we were. Looking back, it seems to me it was all just a case of groupthink in response to the urban legend, coupled with the objects we found. The lack of context heightened the hysteria.

There is however, something very unusual about the land. It is surrounded by other houses, yet it has remained completely vacant for twenty-two years, despite it being situated in an extremely wealthy and busy area. The property is located on Lyons road, which is a major, six-lane, north-south arterial roadway.[4] It is the biggest street in Boca. The area is prime real estate, in a great location, close to the freeway. That is why, even though the evidence says otherwise, I am convinced that there is something very wrong with that plot of land. This property is undoubtedly one of the more peculiar pieces of unknown architectural history.

I know everyone wants a good ghost story, but I didn't set out to write ghost stories. I set out to find the most accurate history of these locations that I could find. There is a silver lining in all of this though—aren't you relieved that something so horribly dark and evil didn't occur there? I certainly am.

Mike E. And me at an abandoned funeral home in 2004.

5

UFO HOUSE

Location: [Demolished] 159 San Remo Drive, Islamorada, FL

HOME SWEET SPACESHIP

The UFO house, built in 1978, was one of a couple of homes designed at the time in this style. Miami architect Peter Vander Klout created it for the Ruzakowski family. While the houses here in South Florida have both been demolished, others still exist today. There is one in Plantation, Florida; one in Garden City, South Carolina; and another in Mettawa, Illinois.

The uniquely shaped, circular reinforced concrete home resembled a UFO. The house was built to withstand winds as high as 300 mph and was engineered to be hurricane proof. The mushroom top section, which weighed over 280 tons, was constructed first, and then it was raised with the use of hydraulic cranes to its final position. Pylons were put under to support the structure, and the walls were then built around the exterior. It was the house of the future, and everything was round. While sturdy and unusual looking, the house's odd shape also made it at times impractical. To get to the bedroom, for instance, you have to go all the way around the house. In the middle, there was a beautiful pool that was ten-feet deep. Guests and friends would dive from the roof into the pool for fun. Unfortunately, the family never really got it remodeled exactly the way they wanted.

Henry Ruzakowski was obsessed with seaplanes. Born in 1911, he emigrated from Poland to the United States around 1920. He started building a life by working in factories building seaplanes. He bought this property intending to fly one of the airplanes he flew in his youth, the Republic RC-3 Seabee. He flew from their house at 159 San Remo Drive in Venetian Shores many times to the shock of neighbors. The lot's location was right on Snake Creek, which leads out to Florida Bay and made it an ideal place to use his Seabee.

Everything had been fine until they started flying the airplane. The residents of Venetian Shores became vocal about their opposition to it for various reasons. The lady next door always complained about the eldest son Henry, a sixteen-year-old, flying the plane.

Some neighbors even spread rumors that the Ruzakowskis were using the Seabee to fly in drugs. For years, the neighborhood Housing Association fought legal battles with them and spent thousands of dollars trying to win. It impaired their enjoyment of the house, but his family had an advantage in the case. The Federal Aviation Administration and the National Oceanic and Atmospheric Administration lent the family legal help to give them the right to use their yard to launch the plane. To appease the neighbors, they stopped taking off and landing on Snake Creek, and instead taxied the aircraft to and from the bay. In the end, they won, and the agencies designated the property a seaplane base, which it remains so to this day.

In December 2012, The Thomas M. Randgaard Trust from Bonita Springs bought the 19,305-square-foot lot for $950,000. Native Construction demolished it in October of 2017.[1] Neighbors were happy to see the house torn down, because it was left abandoned for a long time and was falling apart. Vandals had destroyed what little furniture was left in the house, and it became a place for young people to loiter and have parties. The house was covered in graffiti, and the yard became unsightly and overgrown. The structure outlived its owner though—Henry died in 1998, and his wife in 2013. His children, Henry, Patricia and Edmund are all that remains of its memory.

Left to right Sandra, Denise De La Vega, and me at the UFO house.

6

UNKNOWN CORAL ROCK HOME

Location: [Demolished?] Unknown

THE LOST PHOTO SLIDES

I have no information on this house. I had no memory at first of ever visiting it. The pictures were in a folder containing work I did for my color photography class in 1998. These photos were all taken on Kodak slide film. I was looking for photos to scan, and they were all the way at the bottom, under all the negatives. These pictures are officially my first photos of an abandoned house! Until I found these in January of 2018, I thought my photos from 2004 were my first. It was such a wonderful surprise to discover these images. I was only twenty-one when I took these photos. I have faint memories of the place after seeing all of them. If I find any further information, I will update my website abandonedmuse.com with the story. Also, if this book is ever reprinted, I will make sure to include it as part of this chapter.

TRESPASSING IS A CRIME!
WARNING
This area is a Designated Construction Site and hazardous work area.
The builder / developer will not be responsible for the health, safety, or
welfare of anyone entering this lot or building.
VIOLATORS WILL BE PROSECUTED
BASF
BUILDERS ASSOCIATION OF SOUTH FLORIDA
MEMBER

AFTERWORD

I hope you enjoyed this book. Thank you for letting me take you on the journey through this second installment of *Abandoned Miami*. It took me a long time to pick the houses I wrote about in this book. I wanted to make sure the stories were historically significant and intriguing, as well as important to my readers. Houses are sometimes the most difficult to research because their history is closely guarded by families and hold a lot of personal sentimental value and secrets, but they are extremely rewarding to learn about. Since they are very deeply personal places, I try to be careful when writing about them, because I know there are still relatives out there that once lived in these places and may find this book. These houses were not only full of history, but really beautiful, strange or haunting to explore. I feel lucky to have found them all, and to have had the opportunity to have walked inside to explore and photograph them. As you can tell, they were all extremely important to me and to many others in some way. The memories of these places will be cherished by me for a lifetime. I hope they inspire you to find your own.

Remember to always advocate for your local architectural history and to protect the places you visit. Don't stop fighting for the historic preservation of these local cultural jewels.

Right: Photo by Lissette Ibis Velez-Cuniberti.

ENDNOTES

Chapter 1

1   Motter, Paul. 2007. "Windjammer Barefoot Cruises—The End Of An Empire—Parts 1-4," CruiseMates. November 18, 2007. http://cruisemates.com/articles/luxury/windjammerpt1-111607.cfm.html

2   Carrier, Jim. 2001. *The Ship and the Storm*. New York: McGraw Hill Professional.

3   Motter, Paul. 2007. "Windjammer Barefoot Cruises—The End Of An Empire—Part 2," CruiseMates. November 18, 2007. http://cruisemates.com/articles/luxury/windjammerpt2-111807.cfm.

4   Ibid. Part 3.

5   Herrera, Chabeli. 2013. "Windjammer Barefoot Cruises Founder Michael Burke, 89," *Skift*. May 25, 2013. https://skift.com/2013/05/25/windjammer-barefoot-cruises-founder-michael-burke-dies-at-89.

Chapter 2

1   Leonard, M. C. Bob. 2018. "The Floridians: Florida in the Land Boom of the 20's," Miami: Florida Internet History Center. January 1, 2018. http://floridahistory.org/land-boom.htm.

2   McCaughan, Sean. 2017. "Exploring Al Capone's Fantastically Historic Miami House," Miami: Curbed Miami. July 20, 2017. https://miami.curbed.com/2017/7/20/16003866/al-capone-miami-beach-house.

3   Gomes, Mario. n.d. "My Al Capone Museum," Accessed January 13, 2019. http://www.myalcaponemuseum.com.

4   *The Miami News*. 1928. "Capone Pays $1,200 Interest On Home", October 1, 1928.

5 *The Tampa Times*. 1930. "Gov. Carlton's Arrest Order Held Illegal," April 25, 1930.

6 *The Miami News*. 1928. "Miami District Unites Against Capone Menace," June 28, 1928.

7 *Chicago Sunday Tribune*. 1947. "Al Capone Dies in Florida Villa," January 26, 1947.

8 Medick, Veit. 2012. "Last Living Relative of Al Capone Revisits His Miami Beach Home," *Miami Herald*. November 12, 2012. https://www.miamiherald.com/latest-news/article1942963.html.

9 Ibid.

10 Baumgard, Josh. 2016. "Al Capone's Miami Beach Villa Sells To Sports Agent," Curbed Miami. August 18, 2016. https://miami.curbed.com/2016/8/18/12525046/al-capone-miami-beach-house-mino-raiola.

11 MB Events. 2018. "About 93 Palm," 93 Palm. January 1, 2018. http://www.93palm.com/history.

CHAPTER 3

1 *The Miami News*. 1963. "Orchid Grower Raises Trouble," January 4, 1963.

CHAPTER 4

1 Primera Iglesia Bautista Hispana V. Broward County 450 F.3d 1295 (11th Cir. 2006)

2 Huriash, Lisa J. 2002. "Church Sues County over Zoning Issue," December 6, 2002. http://articles.sun-sentinel.com/2002-12-06/news/0212060019_1_two-other-churches-parishioners-church-s-attorney.

3 Ibid.

4 op. cit. Primera Iglesia Bautista Hispana V. Broward County at 2 (11th Cir. 2006).

CHAPTER 5

1 Goodhue, David. 2017. "This Round House Looked Like a UFO. And Just Like One, It Has Disappeared," November 5, 2017. https://www.miamiherald.com/news/local/community/florida-keys/article182876931.html#storylink=cpy.

BIBLIOGRAPHY

Baumgard, Josh. 2016. "Al Capone's Miami Beach Villa Sells To Sports Agent," Curbed Miami. August 18, 2016. https://miami.curbed.com/2016/8/18/12525046/al-capone-miami-beach-house-mino-raiola.

Carrier, Jim. 2001. *The Ship and the Storm*. New York: McGraw Hill Professional.

Chicago Sunday Tribune. 1947. "Al Capone Dies in Florida Villa," January 26, 1947.

Csnavely0319. 1993. "Windjammer Barefoot Cruise Lines' SV *Fantome* off of Dominica," Wikipedia. January 1, 1993. https://commons.m.wikimedia.org/wiki/File:SV_Fantome_side_view.jpg.

Gomes, Mario. n.d. "My Al Capone Museum". Accessed January 23, 2019. http://www.myalcaponemuseum.com.

Goodhue, David. 2017. "This Round House Looked Like a UFO. And Just Like One, It Has Disappeared," November 5, 2017. https://www.miamiherald.com/news/local/community/florida-keys/article182876931.html#storylink=cpy.

Herrera, Chabeli. 2013. "Windjammer Barefoot Cruises Founder Michael Burke, 89," *Skift*. May 25, 2013. https://skift.com/2013/05/25/windjammer-barefoot-cruises-founder-michael-burke-dies-at-89/.

Huriash, Lisa J. 2002. "Church Sues County over Zoning Issue," December 6, 2002. http://articles.sun-sentinel.com/2002-12-06/news/0212060019_1_two-other-churches-parishioners-church-s-attorney.

Leonard, M. C. Bob. 2018. "The Floridians: Florida in the Land Boom of the 20's," Miami: Florida Internet History Center. January 1, 2018. http://floridahistory.org/landboom.html.

MB Events. 2018. "About 93 Palm," 93 Palm. January 1, 2018. http://www.93palm.com/history.

McCaughan, Sean. 2017. "Al Capone's House". Miami: Curbed. July 20, 2017. https://miami.curbed.com/building/477/al-capones-house.

McCaughan, Sean. 2017. "Exploring Al Capone's Fantastically Historic Miami House," Miami: Curbed Miami. July 20, 2017. https://miami.curbed.com/2017/7/20/16003866/al-capone-miami-beach-house.

Medick, Veit. 2012. "Last Living Relative of Al Capone Revisits His Miami Beach Home," Miami Herald. November 12, 2012. https://www.miamiherald.com/latest-news/article1942963.html.
Motter, Paul. 2007. "Windjammer Barefoot Cruises -- The End Of An Empire - Parts 1-4". CruiseMates. November 18, 2007. http://cruisemates.com/articles/luxury/windjammerpt1-111607.cfm.

Pasley, Fred D. 1930. *Al Capone: Biography of a Self-Made Man*. 1st Edition edition. Chicago: Ives Washburn.

The Miami News. 1928. "Capone Pays $1,200 Interest On Home," October 1, 1928.

The Miami News. 1928. "Miami District Unites Against Capone Menace," June 28, 1928.

The Miami News. 1963. "Orchid Grower Raises Trouble," January 4, 1963.

The Tampa Times. 1930. "Gov. Carlton's Arrest Order Held Illegal," April 25, 1930.

Various. 1970. "Fantome (schooner) – Wikipedia," Wikipedia. January 1, 1970. https://en.m.wikipedia.org/wiki/Fantome_(schooner).